NEKHAU

By the same author:

Bone Ink (2017)
Bone Ink—expanded version (2019)
Our Tongues are Songs (2021)

NEKHAU

RICO CRAIG

RECENT
WORK
PRESS

Nekhau
Recent Work Press
Canberra, Australia

Copyright © Rico Craig, 2022

ISBN: 9780645356304 (paperback)

A catalogue record for this
book is available from the
National Library of Australia

Cover image: Brian McHenry
Cover design: Recent Work Press
Set by Recent Work Press

recentworkpress.com

for Cath
—always another breath—

Contents

FUTURE

Foreword

Love is strong and fragile, slippery and steely. People drown in it, search for it, fight to keep it and yet lose it unexpectedly. This collection asks you to sit with love, to share hopes and fears. We start with fish: protectors, forgotten history, half-selves skimming beneath water's surface, moving mirrors, pieces of sun and star we can almost touch. This collection is full of fish, the real, bodied creatures and their metal cousins—nekhau.

In Ancient Egypt, nekhau were small fish-shaped amulets crafted by jewellery makers and attached to the hair of loved ones as charms against drowning. Belief in nekhau, like belief in most charms, manifested in many ways. There was the idea that the wearer was magically imbued with a fish-like swimming ability and hence safe, or that nekhau hanging in the hair of a loved one would remind them of the water's threat and through this awareness, keep them safe.

Nekhau are laced through this collection, both explicitly and as ghostly reminders. The charms are placed in a contemporary world; poem, voice and words become a way to protect love from threats and fear. These nekhau-poems aim to preserve and shield; they are reminders of dangers near, distant, even imagined, that bear upon our experience of love. Their existence becomes a rehearsal of loss and an expression of hope.

These poems are for the loved and from the loved, in an ideal world you would hear them in the voice of your loved—lovers, children, parents, companions, family all speaking in chorus about the fears and love they carry through the world.

END

golden fish hidden in strands
hanging from waves

Wind chimes

Our hair sways. Where have you been? Are you talking
to river-fish again? Look, I'm the colour of air,
wearing all the clothes you've left,

they're hanging from my shoulders in hollow
swathes. Is that you walking
the street, trouser cuffs dragging, belt hooped

around the bunched waist? Your fingers are ink-
stained; cats and dogs watch you, wild animals
scratch the dirt; sentences drip.

Is there a way to live without our noise? Scuff
a sandy trail, become a street we remember,
build a freeway from breadcrumbs—

I'll do as promised and chant avowals,
plait strands, under, over, word to word. Desire is traffic
rumble without your hand. We're the creatures

we hide in each other. I hear you say, *meet me
at the continent's edge.* We'll make new messages
from broken branches, tumble shells

and rocks into a better truth. I don't remember
the name of this place, sometimes there's a moon
above the passing boats; this must be a shoreline

we know, a harbour we could call memory.
The name must be an incantation, temptation's
teeth marks on a shoulder. I've been gathering

the hands we left hidden in our pockets, words lingering
in lungs, all our parched bones. This is what we promised
to sing, the shape of what we've felt,

each fallible note. If you're not with me I'll carry
your shoes, re-pierce my ears and hang them with the slick
bellies of golden fish. Even when I lose the strength

to speak I'll move like a wind chime,
assailing fate with isobar whorls,
telling our story in the sound of metal upon metal.

And I you

█████████ there are more curls █
to lift from your jacket, teaspoons
████ to stir in ███ coffee.
Later ████████████ afternoon light

██████ against a window. █████████
in the night we've decided to be █ people
██████ we arrange words, carry a spirit level,
dig for the heartbeat hidden in soil.

████ trees outside have been saying █████ winter
████████████████████ August has sweltered;
█████████ we woke to people offering stir-fried
crocodile, █████ we neglected sleep.

████████████████████████████
████████████████████████████

██████████████ you shiver
against four children, every morning

████ shift coals in a fire, warm your hands,
pull fur closer to your throat. ████████████
████████████████ goats are outside
████████████ at night they bramble

through soil, rub against mud walls.
You've built their pen from collected rocks
and wood. Our house is █████ filled with smoke.
████ secret heartbeats ██ inside, we've curtained

the interior into rooms, different lives in each,
████ all familiar with the others'
sounds of love and terror. We know enough
about dreams to block our ears. ██████ at dawn

goats bleat and we move among them
their sides warming our legs, fields full
of grass for their stomachs. ████████████
I lift another curl from the sleeve of your jacket

███ worlds exist in the way it catches light.
█████████ no guns, no money left for violence;
conflict is ████ measured in fists of grain,
we speak of what has been taken to commit war,

what has been wasted to shape metal
into bullets, into the complexity of artillery.
Our hands lift maize and try to read
the kernels ████████ If there was

a homage to you, it would sound
like floorboards creaking, footsteps █████
through darkness, ██████████████████
███ the edge of hearing, the sound of my body

moving toward yours. █████████ voices
in an unfamiliar city, radio,
████████████ news half heard, sounds made
by the last customers to leave a restaurant, then wind

outside, ▮ an awareness of city.
▮ I lift this curl from your sleeve
it tells me ▮ all the lives you have
cared for, people who will never forget

▮ We've decided to fear nothing,
not morning, not the edge of darkness.
You tap a pen against your teeth, wear glasses perched
on top of your head—and these things make me

believe in fauna, flora, flesh. Some mornings
▮ I see you, I ▮ notice ▮ dirt
at the edge of your nails; I hear the tent flap,
voices wailing in the bush, I listen to our singed earth.

Checkpoint

We're leaving glasses around the flat,
condensation in rings

███████████████████████████

on every surface. ███████████████████

███████████████████████████

███████████████████ Effervescence
██████ in every room,
beside the bed, on the floor,
next to chairs. ████████████████████
Most days we brush our hands across succulents
and pretend we know danger, pretend fear is unreachable.
We're distracted by heat haze
murmuring. We argue about small things,
the time of day, the pros and cons of kissing cat paws.
██████████████ Leaves dangle
through the open window.
███████████████ We've been watching
people wave slogans from *The Telegraph*
at empty streets. ████████████████████████
Daughters borrow hats, knot
t-shirts at their side, hide footfalls
as they climb from windows. ████████████████████████

███████████████████████

███████████████████

Four-wheel-drives shudder past, mud-covered,
tin cans rattling from strings, fishing rods tethered
to the roof. People have scratched
'just married' through the dirt. Dogs are loose
in the street. Mangos are 99c each. People nod

at each other when they meet on corners. Bedrooms tell a story
with their dust. The cupboards are empty,
we're all thirsting, pretending the checkpoints are temporary.
Outside the world brays; the sound of shovels
breaking earth, the groan of lawn mowers laying blade
on blade. ██████████████

██████████████████

██████████████████

██████████████████████

██████████████████████

██████████████████████

██████████████████████

Ceorfan

i.

This bus is red. This bus has emergency windows. A handrail. Signs that attempt to prepare passengers for danger. We don't listen to the signs. We test the volume in our headphones. Each person looks away from another. The top level becomes sound. Then void. Then light. Finally voices. They scream at cracked ear drums. Hair has become pollen. There is evidence we were here. The payment on a piece of plastic. Plans in our message bank. The last blip of a phone. Inert metal in teeth. Our frantic DNA.

ii.

It is fever. Water silty with upstream. Animal fur in our mouths. Coughing I cannot escape. I burn myself through night. I let my eyes sink. I exhale the reminder of flame. This is a bed made from husks. I crackle in my sleep. In between words ropes burn my shoulders. An animal rubs against a wall. Bells. Incense. I dream of a thing called ice. Of sugar water. Crushed cane. The residue pulp leaves in a plastic bag.

iii.

Bed clothes have been disinfected. They smell of constricted throat. Nothing is clean. We swallow air through plastic tubes. The membrane across our eyes fills with river water. Vaseline. I know the rain outside better than your face. I know the seagulls when they lose themselves. Metal roofs. Tiled roofs. The illusion of memory. Who are we in this room? Who are these strangers who hold our hands with such tenderness?

iv.

We're covered in ash. Walking naked. Eyes the only reminder of who we are. This is common. To breath filaments that pretend to be air. There are burnings on every continent. Look. Here are the trees we have known. Here are pieces of clothing we have worn until they were reshaped by work. Here are hands that have palmed our chest. The night we swam toward a rip. The babies we promised to suckle.

v.

Humans beat each other with stolen ribs. They pluck the eyes from bodies. They pretend to see. In our blood they run. In our voices. They speak and we hold. The money they hand us. Everything. Printed on air. They touch with the back of knuckles. Each tenderness a threat. We bend around love's shape. Become bells. Become morning's promisee.

vi.

There are many screams. A wave drawing away. Bullet holes plugged with fingers. Ninety planes a day. Lifetimes fish-sided in cargo space. Times four hundred people. Times all the days left on this earth. Equals how many? What can be lettered? Recordings of heartbeats. Dogs roam. Bedrooms already wrapped in dust. After. The question of where this can settle in a body. The lung. The kidney. The secreter of bile. The machine milling food to blood.

vii.

I'm using my hand to eat from a plastic bowl. Maybe tomorrow we will eat dehydrated fruits thrown into a crowd of arms. I will catch. I will chase foil to the ground. There are feet near my fingers. Hands reaching. Dust pressing on my lips. I long for the comfort of cardboard. For the humane promise in electricity. For days when there were animals to slaughter. When the city could breathe at night. There is rubble and dust. Nothing has changed. When we close our eyes the world still disappears in smoke. The streets become grey. Our eyes are made dry—then burn. We fall on our knees and crawl toward family. Toward the next darkness.

viii.

In the morning people knock at the door. My grandmother is brewing tea. Honey in a cup. Tannic welcome. Steam and invocation. We breathe it all. She prays under her breath and I think there is vapour coming from her mouth. She talks about the mountains she will send me from. About boats. Trains. Planes. About walking on a gravel road. How she has buried kin. The better part of a bloodline. How there are trees that drink our blood. How they talk with the cold air. Drop their leaves in streams. How we have already travelled from this place. Our sap. Our nectar. How I will not be the first. That I should run. Take my sister and make friends with the night. Make friends with the sound of city. Befriend the empty space sky offers. We will find bridges to meet on. There will be places where fleeing can cease and still.

broken bone
china of a hurt thing on the verge
the clock ticking beneath ribs

Lullaby

At dawn I held one of our paper babies,
his glue-ridged smile, he blew bubbles about disappearing,
taught me subtraction and division, told me any flight number
multiplied by five and divided by his day of birth
would reveal the coordinates of our first meeting. There's history

in the way heartbeats are collected. Anyone, even I,
could follow coordinates back; see us clad in attentive smiles,
looking for what we didn't know, the one clue
that would warn us. Tonight I'll carry him again,
the message from you written in black ink, folded

in an envelope. I've memorised what he says—listing fears
on paper is a form of protection; I know the lullaby
that tells me where you are, I repeat it
every hour, hoping to learn when you'll return.
I teach him new words we've invented,

tell him there are things free of regret—
horses moving over dust, fast cars, grappa
in underground bars. I don't know if he listens,
if the paper smile is somehow yours. You've started
disappearing when I wake. Every morning

there's a new child. Each time he has a different face,
paper cut creases, tongue jutting from his envelope cheeks;
he winks, knowing the beginning of us—
our thirteen lies, the shape yes makes in your mouth.

Planes landing in the attic

The houses we rent have too many stairs
we're always climbing to attics,
agents call them lofts. We know
what they really are, sometimes we sleep in the empty swank,

mattress on the floor, leeches
cleaning our veins,
surrounded by shopping catalogues, tables dressed in mould.

— boxes—for all the wary words clarifying atrocity,
conversations on hold, questions we'll unravel another day.

...

Dawn comes screeching
through the rooftop. Between us there's air
and sounds humans have placed
in the sky. Soon it will be light,
another day you tell me something
I haven't heard before;
an extra day,
a morning when we know there will not be enough
words to explain the fettle
in this air.

...

In the morning you rub your hair into shape,
measure coffee, talk bananas

from their skins. A bird shrieks
and you speak leaves and branches.
We pack bags, rinse bowls.

...

A temperature we have stopped calling winter
arrives; tiles slide from the roof,
rain on the bed, rain on the—boxes—
planes unceasing, bricks losing their shape,
chains clattering.

Every day is a house
in a street
in a city
in a country
where children are being handcuffed,
made to sit in cells,
locked in the back of wagons.

We will wake wet
as newborns to the sound of other hearts beating,
the world humming around us,
our dreams in all the shapes
we've tried to tamp love into.

...

Vehicles hush in the street outside,
parents' voices push history into new heaps. Teenagers write
their names in blood on windows
hoping there are eyes to read. We place more—boxes—

in the attic. They're filled
with bloody paper, names, the world, all carefully labelled,
brimming. We stack them to the skylight.

fish lift from our blood
fears hunger
make us lace a beloved in amulets

Last time

The cat meows a circle around the cold space
your body makes on the floor. He's right
to be worried. I don't want to pull him away

and admit that someone needs to breathe
life into you. How could I explain
that this time we're going to let you lie?

There will be no calls, no medical compulsion.
I won't hold the phone and plead for speed, this time
we'll be still. Each of us will fill the air around your body

with sounds. I'll touch the shape of your face,
lean toward your neck and make my own feline noise.

Tomatoes promise

I'm watering the tomatoes too much—
again—there's no one
to tap my shoulder
when you're away. Every day I'm out there
sloshing water at the dirt. There's plenty

to worry about; this haze, water
suspended in the air. I've always been
too easy, too willing
to let things ride a little too long. It takes
a firm hand

to propagate. Yesterday I had to kill
a vine covered in black
dust, it took
less than a week to shrivel,
the fruit hanging like green medals.
I cut the dying

away with an old blade,
unknotted it from the tangle
of other plants. When I pulled the stem
from the ground it slid out easily,
roots like discarded hair,

hardly the ligature
needed to draw colour
from soil. Sometimes the life I beg
from seeds forgets to clench, claw-fingered,
to all that is earthly. Instead there are covenants

to be made with loam, streams of air,
with sky and sun.

Heavy Ghosts

Sham ghosts glisten on the whetstone, diatribes hide in every photo,
letters howl at me, books free-fall from the shelves,
shoelaces tie knots in your name. Each record-groove
back-tracks your voice, a Marvin Gaye

summons. I'm trying harder now, when you're not
here, to see, trying for the emptiness people pretend
is peace. I shiver to your favourite songs, stay silent about the ache
that tugs my torso. I'm shuffling the same streets

we walked, half my mind is pretending there are hazards
to step over, my knees quiver. I'm waiting for a cane,
something I can hold in a fist and shake at the world.
They've stopped letting me on the bus, I'm ashamed to say,

most of the drivers know my face, they've seen how I yell
when shadows touch me. I can't bear the cold. They never
know the right thing to say, no one has your voice. For months
I tried to pretend it didn't matter. Now I tell them not to touch

me with their shadows, not to fill the space in my ears
with their half-carved words. Give me better ghosts,
give me a ghost with your lips, let her limp
past me in the morning, offer to make coffee,

search for the sugar. I'll listen and wait for her
to place the mug in my hand. We won't talk about warmth,
about the crushed smile it takes to keep a ghost solid,
the way she climbs on my shoulders when we leave the house,

fills my legs with glorious decades. Each night
when we return home I'll rub liniment
into my ruined knee and thank the empty room
for allowing me to remember our weight.

What we might lose, call her Ingrid

Concrete, cracked edge,
woody roots upturn pavement.
An afternoon shadow surrounded

by blistering light, a peeling heat thrown
across fence and footpath. We have nightmare
clots, the truth beneath our skin. This is the place

where she doesn't look up from the kerb,
where she walks into oncoming emptiness.
Blind sunlight fills the place where shadow

should be. Her voice is a passing car, the rattle
dry leaves draw on wind, pegs falling from a line,
birds shaking branches, buses with uncertain doors.

Even your mother doesn't know her name
or the mottled surface of her baby skin.
Her story is a knot of empty arms—

a necklace, placentas strung on a chain,
clouds between blood and air, years
in the shifting cirrus, a baby cry.

Somewhere in a small city there is a street
and if we look at the fence palings
long enough we might see the place

where her fingers picked at a paint bubble,
dried and lifting from the wood.

a nekhau for every river
for each misty road
each swerve in traffic guided
by safety's intercession

Caverns

When we are one hundred and thirty
pages old and it is still night, you place your hand
on my shoulder and still the shovel I've been swinging

into darkness. This is a place of many walls,
many arms, endless caverns where we are
always at work turning what was into what will be.

Sometimes our chanting becomes sense;
we commit the words to memory, call it lore
and continue. Together we shape night's caverns;

hip-deep in dark dreams, uncut memories splinter
as our shovels strike. We are both bare,
dust in heaving scars on our bodies. Lanterns hang

from pegs on the walls. The turned night is brittle
with words we cannot forget, relic underbellies
china-bone against the dark. We splash

each other with bottles of daylight.
We have been in this place long enough
to talk about swapping skins, digging with another

pair of hands. It seems possible. Our chants continue.
Our shoulders have turned to tender iron.
For hours we fill wooden boxes

with shapes and sift granules of night
though metal membranes. You have said
we must be diligent.

It's no longer possible to recall every word,
we speak in undiscovered constellations. Our breath
is cloaked in granite dust, our lips lifting

above the shroud, bodies distending with air—
we work each lungful.
We are home you say, and I recognise nothing

of this darkness, only artefacts we have collected,
iron we have rubbed across our skin,
treasures you have polished from dust. I clutch

the broken words of our first meeting,
the pens we have handed across tables,
the moments we have been forsaken by maps.

Another day with a pink sun and red moon, another day

we've forgotten there can be orbits. I have
continents in my lungs, each step is a journey
through history. In the park, beneath swings,
astroturf is worn to concrete. At dawn, sleeping bags
air in the sun, the pavement shifts,

when trains pass they're an arm's length away.
The loves of this life have misplaced their promises;
soon we'll join the Gen Xers and what is left
of their baby-fat, camped against the fence, cooking
sachets of noodles over gas burners.

Our new consorts will be measured in the words
that slip between pitched tents. Their doomed
dissection of blame scrapes night
with falling leaves. I dare to fill a bag
with our treasured, useless objects.

For some time I'll remember your name;
your face keeps talking to me and I answer.
We count survivors
and drink instant coffee. The only warm
things are offered like treasures. We are new beings,

documents refuse to tell our story, forms no longer
wish to contain us. When we are directed
it is with amplified voices, with the sound
a baton makes scraping along fence-wire.
We work floodplains during drought,

the beds are dyked, suggesting reason.
We guide trailers through dirt; dry land
is an answer, southern hills
are cold this time of year, abandoned
orchards try to blossom against chill,

nights are defined by the promise of ice.
We wrap ourselves in blankets, talk to smoke
about our old loves, draw
buckets of water from dams and boil them
until what we imagine taints the liquid

has turned to shells and steam.
To remember where we've been we paint
fenceposts green, draw red lines
on old maps, the roads are becoming
thin, curious roots blister through surfaces.

Where fences have fallen, cows trickle
in and out of herds, chewing
grass at the broken roadside.
We've been told to un-memorise
our previous selves, that way has passed.

One thousand hearts

At the next clearing they cook our hearts
on a spit. We sit among what might once have been
walls, now rubble, metal plates balanced
on our knees. Fire crackles. We are hooded

people whispering across the dust. Around us
lives sizzle over fire. Our hawks wait,
restless in the tree behind us,
this is their last night of service. We've died

a thousand times and our hearts
continue to thrash. I still know
the way to your door, which
piece of neon tells the truth.

Our hawks mumble under their shrouds,
we twist the wooden spike, dice the meat,
share it between plates, and hunger
for things alive in each other.

Buildings have turned to vines and leaves,
they varicose away the past, everything
moves quickly, each day
is as hungry as the tropics. What we remember

is becoming green, finding a new face.
We're now leaves twisting
in the weather, vegetal fingerprints
gripping sky. There are ways to live

without a heart, ways to craft a new body from air.

Hawk in my heart

Days are fast and full of hawks. We walk
the streets with hooded companions perched
on our arms. We talk to each other in trills
and chirps, scan the road for rabbits.
As we move through the streets there's colossal
silence, shops are boarded—

the wood is warping, ragged posters tell
the story of long-gone gigs. We pass a pub,
before the bridge over train tracks,
windows are broken—from inside

noise of shapes being dragged
across the floor. The sun sets at noon
and we need to hurry. My old house is a long walk
down Enmore Rd and up Cavendish toward Newington.
The students have vanished, taken by the sun,
burned into the past. Now there's no such thing

as education, gender is hardly recognisable. The survivors
are covered in cloth, our eyes searching
through slits. Now playing fields are pocked
with burrows. What we build will have no destroyers,

there are few of us left to check dates—none
who will remember names. We tell each other
about the times we needed pens, how we collected
words, how there were objects used for writing
and our tongues were limber with love, infatuation,
squandered language. Our hawks stretch their wings;

their feathers pop at the air, they amplify
toward flight, we lift their heads and they sharp-eye
tussocks in the field. They're disdainful of a world that refuses
to unknot prey. We feel them rise from our arms,

an aria beaten to gold, a weight
disappearing, they lift into the last of light.

witching history's kinks
searching for ways
to make us unassailable

After life

At world's end I will carry a tent, I will have the best
of our secrets sewn into a sleeping bag. The mettle
your body has deserted will take my hand
and lead me away. Everything will be cold.
The machines attending your arms will be silent
and all the things we have done
will become mine alone. As protection I'll write
them in the air, I'll bury our stories beneath
the only trees still living, scatter them on empty
streets, let hot winds lift them. People will swerve
from my path as I walk by. I'll sleep in a blanket
of coughed words, chew scraps that gather around me,
fill my mouth with memories and sew myself to sleep.

In the humid afterlife, in the belly a tent makes
beneath sky, you will hum and it will be possible
to hear your body, and all the sounds
our life was filled with, press against mine.

neon embolus (i am inside i am)

each day is neon-bound—you know
we listen to the sound earth makes under stars
your name has hollowed my ears
everything is riddling

to your shape—trumpets wail
there's fruit in a white bowl
when i mention you—street lights know
and windows rattle
who you are—i talk to every shiny surface—say

inside my brain are words
written in neon—twisting letters trying
to remind me of the things i have already said
or mean to say
glowing
scrolling
giddily formed

…

i am also inside my brain—tongue in my hand
i watch myself steal stems
from every letter—collect the curves
from vowels and rebuild
sounds

shapes
become new words—become sentences
become the hiccups of knowing

...

i try to tell you the same story
the unmowed verge is golden and swaying—
when i empty to fill silence
my best words are torn sheets
broken windows—a dog's howl
i try to tell you
when we're fifty we'll climb on a roof together—
we'll have dirty feet
it will be night— the tiles will be wet
our fears will be tucked in clouds

you listen with your editor's eye
trying to seal the echoes
before i turn them into new things—we have time
we have only
brume's uncertain brink

...

i have forgotten—i am the person
with a tongue
all my neon sifted
for rage and muddle—the body carrying me
a mouth full of knots pretending to be words

you sit on the edge of our bed and see
my hands shake
your eyes are a clock face—your iris
becomes afternoon light and foliage

...

each day i try to tell you the same story
how the city fell from our sides
how mosquitoes flew in silence—and i know
my voice sounds like a gargle
and when i tell you about the harbour and our feet
on a sandstone ledge
i know
it sounds like i'm calling for a nurse

and each day i try to tell you the same story
each day i try to tell you

everything is riddling
your name has hollowed my ears
we listen to the sound earth makes under stars
each day is bound in neon—you know

NEKHAU

Nekhau

My arms stretch transparent to reach you, I'll plait your hair in messy clumps,
golden fish hidden in strands,
hanging from waves.
My hair is already jangling with your words.

where you are   there's a river edge   maybe a rock ledge   land taken by tide
almost submerged   days are stippled with dreams   filled with sun   water
pepper trees   buckets of crayfish
impending rain

I've carved a pocketful of nekhau, catfish with bellies of light,
smaller than fingernails, each dorsal detail etched into gold.
I want to send so many they'll press delicate warnings
into the thrill of your hairline.

I've been witching history's kinks,
searching for ways to make us unassailable.
Wisdom says we should catch fish
as they swim upside down at dawn,
their oyster-shell bellies kissing sunrise, that we should make
golden replicas and fill our pockets
until they bulge, bead our hair with tiny
fish shapes to float our heads safely above waves.

At Sydenham Station I drift like Synodontis batensoda, upside-down,
my face tilted to sky. Trains drag
cross-currents along the platform. For weeks you've been aiming stories
across oceans. Planes cant from clouds. I wish your face into every window,
you're due soon or it might be weeks. I've been side-eyeing specifics—waiting.

These trains
have their vows. I point my toes at the sound metal makes
on metal, my fingers working our words
into fish-shaped amulets. I've been chewing my tongue
into a hex, something hot enough to forge
charms from your keystrokes.

Fish lift from our blood,
fears hunger, they make us lace
a beloved in amulets. Here, there's only
the smell of rail tracks,
the electric current, diesel
and the Cooks River as my slow-moving Nile.

Fears make safety a barren space, they press cold
lips against our bare teeth, remind us that we know the broken bone
china of a hurt thing on the verge,
the clock ticking beneath ribs;
endings are a lightning strike, a blown tyre, the moment of inattention.

It's worked until now. I know the novel you're reading,
the song as it slips from your lips; exactness lifted
from each day. Air finds a way to sound your name:
voices on the radio telling me to put crayfish to sleep before they're boiled
and all I think about is you
licking pepper sauce from your fingers.

Can you hear the seismic clunk gold amulets make when you run,
feel the extra weight secret in your hair? A nekhau for every river, for each misty
road, each swerve in traffic guided
by safety's intercession, an extra breath
when you slide under water.

Early

Some days your fingers cramp
around a steering wheel, you rat-run
for hours through narrow streets, eyes
attuned to the city's précis. Trucks pass,

rubbish skids from bins, bus drivers
drift across lanes, horns
sound. It will be another day
when the sun ascends where it should and sets

over a tree I could point to. In the afternoon
people will walk dogs and argue
with children. Sometimes you work
in a tatty souvenir shop near the Quay,

handing tiny koalas to tourists. You roam
streets with an extra body and three tongues
of new language. On a day I'll have only one reason
to remember—you will leave your other

life five minutes early, somewhere you will run
for a train, a stranger will hold the door
and nod as you sneak through.
You will walk along a street in the city where I live.

A water pipe will be spilling its heart, a woman in a yellow vest
will direct you across the road. Clear water will stretch
across the street, gutters will fill, courier bikes will
have an ocean above their rims, the water in a city block

will be turned off, jack hammers will start. I will be
sitting on a bench. It will be Wednesday. I will be watching
the water pass and waiting for you to appear.
Everything continues without us, timetables

are petty. At night when we fold ourselves
into bed, we whisper in other continents. My hands
beg for a third night of love. We wait for our bodies
to arrive. Sometimes I am beside you with nothing

rough on my face, the grey has been forgotten
by my hair. I am looking at you with eyes
of one colour. On those nights your curls slack
into promise, your neck twists like the coast of Java;

we're under a mosquito net, snakes have made
a home in the ceiling, there's bamboo
in our hair, fronds wishing against each other.
In this place we wait to be inflected by desire.

We remember marriage proposals we want
to forget, boyfriends who cry themselves to sleep.
Even our blood runs in new ways,
arteries awash in neon noise. Futures lurch

into thought and we curl in hallways locking
ourselves together, believing if we stare
at each other long enough, it will be possible to see
all the bodies we can be rise from our eyes and walk.

catfish with bellies of light
smaller than fingernails
each dorsal detail etched into gold

Chalmers St, three flights up

From an open window, three flights up, we yell
into our city's spine; bristle and tongue,
street lights bend to us. We love like brigands,

eat with bent forks in a half-furnished flat, blow
promises out the window and watch them settle.
We kiss the face of every fear; your hair

is jewelled with swaying catfish,
they're breathing the days we carve
for each other. We are two bodies and this room

has become every city. We imagine harms, pretend
to be love-safe, protected. On the nights
we steal, I wait for you to return to our open window.

In the alley below people search bins, phones flare
and disappear into pockets, clouds
make allegations. You've started to hum

in your sleep, a tune that exists in the river
your mind becomes at night; your dreams
drifting, golden with fish, on street sounds.

What keeps people from the water

on the beach a chanting casuarina
wind-plotting tomorrow's dunes
our intentions pressed into each dormant heartbeat
shells remember

driftwood has legs and scales
we give the water our toes
two unwashed ankles
we don't talk about the marks made on sand

branches and fallen trees
have started to run for the water
tails swinging for balance
no one swims here

not this time of year
when we emerge from under the casuarina
our cheeks are scrimmed with white sand
all along the beach we hear

evolution's arcane sound
crocs furrowing waves
salt water slick over snouts
animal glare in their veins

we see the knife-curve young crocs leave
a scratch of claw
each tail-touch a deft slash on damp sand
and we tumble into white water

Dress in skin

Our wrists are bound in bite marks,
we hold them toward the sun,
dress our fingers in sand.

I have the feeling we're almost done
with clothes, we've been naked for days;
talking to the sheets, communicating

in creases, binding
ourselves in strands of hair. Skirts are a lie
you've stopped telling, you've forgotten

the word for dress,
the language we speak
is skin, fingernails on the edge of a tongue.

When tomorrow comes it is almost
always dawn's lilac haze.
We sleep under a net; skillets float

in the sink. At midnight
we make pacts with night-animals
as they appear at the window. I've promised

them your first words and a memory
you wouldn't share. All they've bartered
is another crescent of light, three

slices of polony. There are days when the past
returns with each breeze, when the future
tightens and the ants crossing our feet

always bite, when we are hackled
with different lifetimes. Others
when we are only skin to mouth,

hands full of all we know about
each other and the nights are stone fruits,
tender, waiting to be eaten, and we become

lips, tongue, working flesh from seeds.

Fiat 128

On wind-riddled nights you fill the bed with cars,
Fiats and their overwhelming engines, gears pushing
against your palm. Your arms shudder through revolutions.
The wind loves your face and you're surrounded
by cracked leather. Sometimes the petrol gauge floats

forever, just above empty. You're alone at the wheel,
it's almost morning, the Doctor is still in, each ripple
on the Indian Ocean is topped with a wrinkle of white down.
Sand hides under your fingernails, an expanse
unbuckled in your mind, the night draws an arm

over his face, turns. The road is hedged with purple.
You slow the car. The ocean draws back
into itself. An empty space talks
beside you. We can love what carries us
away and back. Your hands grip

the wheel like a future you've started to know.
Gears find their place, waves push another curve
toward shore. The world brims with tiny seditions;
there are arms in your mind, the scent of olives
in the morning, your chest is valve, piston, full of words—

Earlwood mansions

I'm still building our house in Earlwood,
a mansion with no roof or door, on the cliff face,
windows open to the river. There's a room scattered
with buoyant thoughts, our chit-chat,

a floor that always needs sweeping. I place sunlight
on surfaces, maybe whistles from the playing fields,
dogs barking, hardly any cars on the road below.
Some mornings we wake before dawn to watch

the river. When our children rise, they're adults;
we offer them coffee, pile a table with fruit,
slide jugs of water. Maybe a decade has passed,
it's unimportant. The light feels more

saturated; I've lost an eye to something
that will pass, you've grown your hair. We knew
there would be a place to hold all we created
in other lives, children, dry fingers tangled

in our hair, the pages in our hearts, days
we carried chairs to dinner parties and fell into beds
with wine glasses in our hands. Undercliffe scarp
hoards all our river patter. Every afternoon

grasshoppers spring from the table
edge and tumble through an open window
searching for sunset. In the fading light,
we cook, we promise to stay strong.

make golden replicas
and fill our pockets until they bulge
bead our hair

In the kitchen singing love songs

The kids we love digitise each strut and vape exhalation,
brush labels from their bodies, fluff their hair,
hang leather braids from their wrists. They speak
with lizard tongues, carry watermelon-flavoured gum,
line their pockets with smoke machines. Some days

they're a stretched canvas, they talk about conspiracy
theories, photo filters and spiritual cleansing. We wonder
what we're missing, all this scented smoke,
feet with their toes turned in, profile names
minacious as broken glass. Every conversation

sounds like an audio recording—a memory of ages
already past. Valedictions are once only, everything disappears
before we have a chance to listen again. They make new acronyms
for love, for the best way to shape eyeliner. Their words
seem more real than the whole of history. We watch eels

escape their mouths, all the letters slippery, longing and fast
between our fingers—
What they've borrowed from us could slide
through the eye of a needle. They twist and turn
in a bed, grin shards and rearrange

pixels every morning when they wake.
Somewhere ahead they will eschew all objects
coated in plastic, stop breeding, fasten their fists
around what is sharp; declare life to be
the sound static makes roaring at golden hour.

Our dog is a river

Our dog refused the name we gave her. She only
turned when you beckoned with the names of rivers.
We spent hours searching maps, testing new creeks,
trying to find worthy water. At sunset you riddle
the sky with tributaries—Dyarubbin, Hunter, Darling.

On sleepless nights we convene in harbour parks.
I carry an old tennis racquet
we got from a junk shop. You stand beside me
as I lob the ball into darkness. Wherever we are
the sky is clear and filled with shapes we recognise

from other nights, constellations we've plotted before.
The dog runs across wet grass, rolling, turning,
snuffling through longer tussocks, returning
to place the ball at our feet. I aim another lob
at nothing, it arcs into darkness and falls

where it should, where it always would. There are
movements that can be predicted, end points known
from the force exerted, from the shape and weight
of the object leaving. In the sky there are bodies, longing,
always returning, their trajectory manifest

against darkness. To believe, we fill the air
with earth-sounds: a ragged chase,
river-mewl, consonants of loved ones. Each night
our dog turns, fur riddled with dead grass,
eyes full of stars, mind churning her river.

Memory's blade

Bareback country, nights cold enough
to hear the sound of my grandfather
chopping wood. His true swing,
his faulty eye. There are histories
I haven't told you, axe wind we never speak of,
I'm not sure there'll ever be time.

No stars tonight, only hard rain
and mud along the fence line. We sling
our phones on the verandah to ice over,
each morning they're slick and forgetful.
In this world we learn to be creatures of earth,
we grow hooves and muscle tangles

from the ground. Sun slants through the bare
branches of an apple tree. You lie naked,
calling each morning from clouds. This sunrise
is layered with ice. No one visits these orchards.
Woodsmoke wraps around us, we wander
room to room, bowls of beef bourguignon

in our hands. Outside, the sound cold air
makes against metal, the sound grandfathers make
against your heart. I load logs onto the flames.
We hide in a smoke-filled room,
gather fallen branches and stack them by the fire,
drink wine on the floor, cover our hands

in ash. Over the hill, we are four-legged again,
galloping through bush, the ground drumming
under our stride. Each day we hurtle
into a gorge, air echoing. Our mouths squall
sounds animals use to exhale fear.
This fire burns. We'll grow

throat-bound and speak with a rasp.
I hear that axe every time we step from the door,
wind is loyal around the blade,
and my Pop wore family like a battered
pair of thongs, his foot cut cloven
by his commitment to the blade's

pristine edge. We'll fill this fire with fallen
branches, burn them back
to the sky. Maybe I'm sending messages.
We don't sign our name anywhere,
when we leave the only remains are embers
we have abandoned. These are the first days

we are free; we could stay in this deserted orchard
watching what we have become. The ice
on branches, sound streaming from our lips,
hearts ready as splinters, fruit
cradled within our beckoning arms.
I try to say what I learned from him—how to walk

blind and shirtless in the scrub
by the rail line, whipped with sunflowers,
hole in my throat croaking
about the love we longed to return.

Daughters attach themselves to dust particles

You'd weave fingers for your daughters, braid
yourself new dreams. In now's clarion

you could reveal. Confess yourself empty. Leave
them the riddle of a vacant body. Would they recognise

the missing, the secrets of you? Daughters, hands warm
with other blood; they know the hardest questions.

They ask when love starts, when love ends. It could be
a question or knowledge. Answers are as difficult

as extracting air from water. They farewell us
with a forearm behind the neck, each goodbye is a heart

saying nevermore; for weeks we hear their voices through a phone,
read messages. They could be standing across the road,

chorusing their own legacy with made-from-night friends,
singing about becoming in darkened parks. They're always

changing plans, finding new reasons. We talk about them,
wonder where they'll sleep. I noticed one yesterday

riding a motorbike, changing lanes without indicating.
She mazed her way through traffic to New Canterbury Road,

a shape sliding between lanes, tail light flaring.

Black Swans

When we meet mist comes with us, entering
windows, filling beds, holding court with other
equivocal elements. One afternoon we're above
ourselves, with pale clouds within us
blowing across the river; buildings disappear,
ferries are hidden, and we are outside
our bodies, loose on water, spread thin
enough to walk through. You know these shores
better than me, the threat of dry-cold,

Federation detailing in the suburbs, the afternoon wind.
There's white in front of our eyes and we're sweeping
around gates you've seen before, stirring through the gaps
between door and doorframe. I see you fill the shoes of people,
weave desire's voice into forgotten clothes—a vapour telling
hearts to beat. Strangers breathe us into their lovers,
carry us place to place. There are old friends drinking
at Seven Stars, we drift through the open door,
breathe bubbles into champagne, make sirens call

for their mirror. Outside the late trains carve through our mist,
buildings lift chins above us, planes circle, hypnotised.
The river is a misshapen question and we answer, waking,
white air, the love beneath an eyelid. Our molecules crush
against pale ether; our songs float on water, fill culverts,
push against the scarp. All night we protect the rocks,
hide them in our sleeves; and when sunrise wakes us,
we lift from earth. I'm floating above the bed,
beside you, in a half-dream light shines into. My ears are filled

with sounds—lungs expanding, the river expelling life.
There are shapes hidden below our skin and each morning
I remember you as clearly as blood remembers a vein.
Love is cellular, in the sky, and you are still beside me. We will rise
and move into the day, encased in the people we are; we will drift
from this place, there will be buses to catch, clouds to be;
and for a moment it is impossible to know what has become of *me*,
become of *you*, if there is an *I*. It's possible the scientists
have been truthful and we are clouds of swirling

matter, and only our pact with vision keeps us solid.

Fennel

We stand, elbow-touching, thin-slicing fennel,
squeezing lemon. You use a potato peeler
to sliver parmesan. This salad
has been working for days, years. I agitate
the oil and lemon. A breeze blows
through the open window, dry as branches
covered in sea salt. We breathe carefully.
I reach for some bread, we don't speak,
there's the sound a knife
makes against crust,
the waves,
wind on leaves,
first cicadas.

Our nights are a stage

We've been learning magic tricks together
talking about places to hide,
marking the walls we might emerge from.

I go to the kitchen and you're already there; curled
in the cupboard beside the plates, wearing
a top-hat and tails, passing wine glasses

and waving me back to the party. In the other room
people talk about trees
and the number of pixels in each photograph.

I could believe in your body, bent to the cupboard's shape,
glass in hand, knees tucked to your chest,
finger pressed on lips. Maybe there's magic

only I know. Before each trick you show your palms
to the audience, turn out your sleeves, promise
all is as it seems. My clumsy hands and T-shirts

have vanished. I slide myself into a glitter gown,
smile at a darkened room, step into a box,
let myself be cut into parts, wrists bound

in chains, blindfolded, wait for the audience to cheer
as my ears fill with water. Each night
your suit jacket coils to the floor, I loiter

in the emptiness between tricks, waiting
for the incantation that makes me reappear.

Ragnar Kjartansson in Bre

What I should have said is—it snowed once
in Bre
and only the kids with bitten fingernails noticed; for half a day
we stayed with curtains drawn
exhaling our backing music.

The storm left geologic hairlines: three photos
hidden in a digital drawer,
shape of a key in my back pocket,
the sound of water before
it froze beneath our feet.

What I should have said is—things we know are neonate,
a new moon birthed by trees, first embrace floating.
Our children are stars exploding,
sons who never come home for lunch,
daughters who call too early in the morning.
I've heard you, nighttime-lucid, give them
new names. They don't listen to anyone
except us. Mostly we sing

songs recorded in bath tubs, under open sky
with broken guitars and foot-stamp percussion.
I don't know if that's the optimal soundtrack,
but our sons and daughters sing along
and the words that come from their lips
are promises stretching across space.

What I should have said is—when the Fish Traps iced up,
people stayed at the Club
and didn't know why; snow drifts
were halfway up the glass doors,
the smoking area abandoned,
there was nothing but white-collar country
on the big screen. Drinks were served
without ice, all
we had to eat were salt and vinegar chips.

What I should have said is—when children open the curtain
streets will disappear. In this sunset
- visitor - will have fifty-six meanings,
another future will walk to the Traps,
history will be rock and ice.
Across the frozen shallows
the only sound will be water cracking.

What I should have said is—when we leave the river will thaw
fish will return to sinewy purpose, water will
wear away ice
water will work a path between rocks.

Hooves of Taurus

I'd curl with the grass for you, bead my brow
with worn stones, call them constellations,
drag them nightly across your vision.

There are manes in the sky moving with love,
borne each night with aeons in their eyes, cluttered
in a celestial groove hoping to be renamed. Their dots cluster

into intimate astronomies; these are shapes we need to mark
on a rock face, carve their light into amulets,
set them in patterns we can squat over, messages we can read

with the soles of our feet. For now, we will be still, we'll fast
on minutes, dry-tongue stars on skin, lie across each other
recreating constellations we've borrowed from the sky.

You rest a hand on my face and somewhere above Orion canoes
in dark space, travellers hold a skillet to the moon's edge
& Taurean hooves pound strands of lost hair

into tomorrow's light. Let's listen to the sound
we make under stars, feel the way our ears hollow
so they have space to hold the moment when we say—

I am matter, here with you, golden scales.
We will talk until the Milky Way lingers
in lake-water, until the Panhandle knows the moon

& spiders build their webs, until dew settles
& the sun lifts to sharpen each droplet
& we will talk until what we have said

finds a place in all that is blue.

FUTURE

Don't smile for passports

Confounded tourists, dust clouds,
coalesce. Cars perch
in my blindspot, they have number plates
I remember from before. T-shirts are new

again, when you arrive we'll talk about memories
we've stowed in formaldehyde, compare maps.
Until then my favourite advice is from smokers
as they flick cigarette butts into space.

Today, gravity has another purpose,
it makes planes land, it holds our feet
to the ground, plants buildings for us
to meet in. When you arrive we'll float

into rooms we already know; tables plotted over baths,
no windows, we'll look in wardrobes
for bathrooms, talk to each other until our lips are lined
in code. The plaza will be full of wooden tables, birds,

an edifice holding sunset, times we've forgotten
to talk about. I'll wait for you near the place
where cats line the wharf. When you arrive,
remind me—there'll be light and tomorrow and time.

Rain on the Seine

Imagine it never stopped raining. If the Seine rose from its bed and streamed into streets. If we stood on Rue des Barres with water welling over our ankles.

I'd have a shopping bag beneath my arm, we'd both be under your umbrella, it would be as postcards make us believe.

Even then, we wouldn't be able to tell people what we'd seen.

Imagine if there were churches burning at midday.

Imagine if the water kept rising, if the Metro started to fill, if stairways became waterfalls and low-lying museums were forced to usher people out, to turn on alarms, if all the attendants were pointing toward assembly areas, if nothing was a drill.

We've seen all these things.

We bite our lips, hold every secret in our lungs.

Waiters knee-deep in river water, standing on the terrace, sipping coffee, pining for diners to return. Skulls somehow floating from catacombs, grinning at clouds. Mondrians and Braques drifting past, a Valadon wrapped in net. If the rain never stopped every drop would stay in this silent place, no cars, no pedestrians, only water and stone, new currents hidden in the world behind our lips.

fingers working our words
into fish-shaped amulets

Melichloro

We pull over to the gravel roadside,
the thirst of scooters has grown familiar,
our hands shudder. We've been following
hillside curves, looking
for the right stone building

to stop near, to wait beside.
Mist is knitted to the Aegean,
it could be clouds stretching
from their home. Ships could float
on this air, myths could storm

across the white wash. The sun
begins to come through.
I can hear birds and what I believe
is the sound an ocean makes. There are fish
out there, squid, plankton; slippery

meanings that have escaped.
We're haunted by pale creatures twisting
in tidal silence, taunting the myths
that live above water. The ships
move toward us. My heart is white flesh—

you reach an arm around me
and lean toward my shoulder; the mist
lifts a little, the ocean grows. In this place
we eat only hard cheese, in chunks
from a knifepoint. Inside buildings

there is shadow, thick-walled, cool and quiet.
We meditate watching olives in brine.
I have familiar sand between my toes,
the grit knows my story better than me.
Soon men will arrive and compare cigarette

papers; four words will be spoken, stories
carved on the table. If I close my eyes
there is history in the divots, slashes
that I haven't learned to read. I think
of cave paintings, I think of the way

precarious lives become permanent—
the way we try to mark ourselves
into veneer and call it art. My finger rubs
the table surface, it reminds me of picnic tables
in forgotten parks, of kids

with pocket knives and time to spend scratching—
how we are other people
even here on another continent
where history is another name, a distant relative
who took time to cherish a mound of stones.

Two flights up at
92 Linnaeushof, Watergraafsmeer

Today we ravished a canal. You were waiting
foot on a boat's prow, dark, flat water at your back.
We were stones ready to skim. I started loving you
again at breakfast when you opened a notebook
and began drawing pictures of all the people

we'd promised not to mention. For five days we've lived
like runaways, kissed in a haze of minor crimes.
We press our ears to hotel bannisters and wait
for misdemeanours to drum in our ears. Stairs creak
the three names we've hidden

our love behind. In this city you'll tell me
how you lost your finger, who left the scar
beneath your fourth rib, the gristle in the eyebrow
above your third eye. We skip across water;
there are freighters, cargo ships, cruise liners. People balance

bicycles on boats. The sun is steady and we are always
delinquent with desire. Strangers try to tell us where to eat,
they say we should stomach nothing but plants. We stay
and let the seasons change around us, trams become
new shapes, we move into a terrace outside old town;

the streets are wider, there are no tourists. Every day you start
work at a wooden table, take a single pen from the drawer.
I watch you write biographies of women

you wish you'd known. Your notebooks are full
of unexpected meetings. I listen as you retell tales,

point to places you had coffee with portrait painters,
ate cheese with physicians. Word by word our suburb
fills with ghosts of the good and great. They wait patiently
to speak to you again. I stand beside you, sunlight
discovers the wall, our roof is too high to clean, a spider web twists.

We listen. Each morning is carved from a piece of glass.
Today we walk beside the canal, watch for people who are new
to this place, if they've lost their way you'll pull
a pen from your pocket and write our secrets on their fingers.
The only place we age is on museum steps,

drinking plum brandy in the moonlight,
searching strangers' fingertips for all we left.
It's always late July with a sun too busy
to set, we can hear water making promises,
voices answering. In this life, schools are abandoned,

repurposed as restaurants, we dance
in warehouses that smell of earthmoving
equipment and fertiliser, our shoes are covered
in oil. All we want for is cigarettes, cities
to brush our hands over, cobblestones

to speak with; I've been making promises
on WhatsApp again, riding canal boats with Italians.
I know you hear the other voices, we let our minds
stray. There are nights it's enough to be disheveled;
your top lip always tastes of slivovitz, bartenders

wish us only joy. There'll be a time
when all I want is another day in a port city,
in Watergraafsmeer or any suburb where you held
an ear to my chest. But that is years away,
those fingernails haven't scratched air. Now we watch

people line the streets for waffle cones, admire
the boats, so low they almost forget to float.

Electronegativity

A dog crosses the road; small, interior, a shape
to be perched on a pillow. You watch
from our window, lower your pen,
close your notebook, begin to stand. The dog turns,

sits—stranded on the tramline. Our street is deserted,

morning quavers with winter wind. Fur shivers
as the dog curls into a ball. You stand.
We're both watching. Linnaeushof is empty,
trees move, the dog's fur lifts. We're about to speak;

trees shift shadows on your table. The door slams

and I can imagine you in the stairwell,
without a jacket, bare feet, running. When I see
you enter the frame our window creates
your hair is wilder than I remember, lifting

with each step. The dog is a bundle of brown

fur breathing. Tram tracks gleam
to the next intersection. I notice motion:
trees moving, paper tumbling,
distant lights changing, a scooter crossing

the intersection. Concealed by day-to-day, elements steal

electrons from each other and become
new selves. You reach the dog and kneel. It leaps,
pawing at your chest. You stand, feet naked, wind re-shapes
your hair, the dog has rounded to sanctuary. You look up;

in our window is a familiar, moving behind glass.

The Visitors

We dwell in a single room,
near walls of jasmine, close to sky. Life lingers
in our shadow. On the hillside—
red shapes might be flame trees

or other days. Our phones vibrate. Birds
stutter. You pass me old travel cards, insects
celebrate under leaves, oysters gush
from every rock. We watch friends

shuffle down hallways. A tin roof, wind. Push
my face to one side and lean closer. At night
ants walk scent trails
along our arms, we wake to plastic bottles

rolling across the wooden floor, sky splayed
on the kitchen table. We count
mosquito bites and shift fans;
travel room to room in search of clothes,

our hands are slandered with life. We live
on tap water, raw almonds, pieces of carrot
shaved into curls. Out the back, bats eat unripe peaches
and scare in leathery bundles whenever we trip

down the steps after midnight. It makes sense to us,
this disposition; days when the sky brims
with water. Keys are lost. We communicate
in fallen ferns, shucked bark, seeds,

when we chatter it sounds like broken shells.
This should be written in sand at the water's edge,
so when people look there's nothing
to possess; only a pattern we say

lives in a particular kind of light. We listen
as people talk about children, sisters—the years.
Our bats are singing. We're nodding to each tune,
leaving eye lashes on every surface,

straightening sheets until they hold us again.
Tonight we'll play old disco records
slide our feet from shoes, dance across floorboards
and tell our visitors it's time to leave.

an extra breath
when you slide under water

Can you stay?

Any noise could be the promise of you arriving;
the wash and thunk a boat makes docking,
roping to wharf, hull bumping worn tires.

You've drawn by my side on a motor bike,
two-stroke slapping the air. Other times, on a skateboard
—languid glide added to your stride. Once you arrived

at the footy oval under Earlwood Rise steering a tuk-tuk.
Right now I'm expecting the click a playing card
makes in a spoked wheel, you rounding the corner

on a BMX I owned in the 80s. I don't know where
you found it, how you managed to tighten the chain.
I'll ask what I always ask, *How long can you stay?*

You'll touch my face, chain-grease on your fingers,
smear a trail of prints as you try to remember
my name; let our bike roll into the river as you kiss me.

Three fingers to my lips

I would kiss you again

Your gate has clattered, bins line the footpath,
bells cascade from the fence

but I have to leave

our other selves have been watering the pot plants,
conducting mosquitoes

and I'll return

around a huntsman. When you bring three fingers
to your lips I know it is mangle and promise:

I would kiss you again

we're tattooed by train lines, electricity,
plenitude, inequity buried in a jingle-jangle.

but I have to leave

Trees have relinquished crown and leaf-rustle,
now bollards grow from the ground,

and I'll return

cars scrape against each other,
crimple your name in narrow alleys.

I would kiss you again

Your love orbits each letterbox,
Your love echoes on a mouth, weaves through wire mesh.

but I have to leave

Deserted trains know our footsteps,
we watch the sun set in broken windows.

and I'll return

When you put an arm around my neck
you feel the golden in my hair, the shimmer-fin;

I would kiss you again

and those syllables hugging us close
become jumble in our lungs.

but I have to leave

When you touch my face I know it means
there are places we'll arrive together.

I would kiss you again

When you bring three fingers to your lips
I know it means—

I'll return

Ligature

Pull me toward you, the wind is blowing, light hammers
our strings. I can hear trees swaying sinuous names.
At your doorstep there's another night, beyond,
morning air. We lean closer and we are arms,

strings tuning to the present. Your tongue
on my teeth is telling stories. I feel a one-act play,
a saxophone. Your nose is a festival against my cheek.
This sunset is drenched amber. Tonight rain

will fall, this southerly will soothe us. It's possible
to see a future where the salt in us makes our tears
soft; where we never become wasted things, the semaphore
of our beckonings beating against empty air, where all the metal

in our bodies will help us float. Who thought we'd stand
at your front gate? Who dared imagine
the merciful groan as it opened with the breeze?
The veins in our bodies listen and move, piano wire

hidden beneath our skin, shimmering
with sounds. We write sonatas leaning
against this tree, waiting for night to appear. Your voice
coils around me and I am cradled

in steel threads, copper strands dangling
from my fingers. In this future we face each other
jangling, tiny, metal gills beating morse against our jugulars,
scales shivering to the rhythm of each pulse, kissing

as the setting sun hammers our strings,
breathing as wind folds branches around us.

Acknowledgements

I respectfully acknowledge that this book was written on the land of the Gadigal and Dharug people.

All my gratitude to the wonderful editors of the publications where these poems first appeared, often in earlier, more ragged, forms: *Australian Poetry Journal* and *Australian Poetry Anthology*.

Brian McHenry—

much appreciation for your willingness to put up with rambling zoom calls from the other side of the world as we blethered through ideas about the cover. What you came up with was a wonderful surprise. Thank you for seeing the heart of this collection.

Felicity Plunkett—

you were handed a manuscript that would have horrified a mere mortal. Of course you didn't falter! Thanks for your always generous and perceptive handling of these words.

Shastra Deo and Sam Roxas-Chua 姚—

two poets whose work I respect deeply, thank you for being early readers of this collection.

Shane Strange—

thanks for taking me into the Recent Work family and showing astounding faith in the early days when this was more an idea than a collection.

kylie—

thanks for your strength and all the days.

pax—

swim far, swim in the light, tumble in the white water

Bilal Hafda—

honestly your belief in poetry hones my belief in a way that is hard to express. Always great to do the work of writing alongside you. Your collection is coming, we both know it!

Cath—

for innumerable readings, for endless patience with the wrangling of this collection, for never doubting, for all your love. Thank you. May the nekhau always swim for you.

About the Author

Rico Craig is a writer, award-winning poet and workshop facilitator whose work melds the narrative, lyrical and cinematic. His poetry has been awarded prizes or shortlisted for the Montreal Poetry Prize, Val Vallis Prize, Newcastle Poetry Prize, Dorothy Porter Poetry Prize and University of Canberra Poetry Prize. *Bone Ink* (UWAP), his first poetry collection, was winner of the 2017 Anne Elder Award and shortlisted for the Kenneth Slessor Poetry Prize 2018. Since 2012 he has worked as Storyteller-in-Chief at the Story Factory, designing and facilitating creative writing programs for young people, and teacher development programs for adults. *Our Tongues Are Songs*, his second collection of poetry, was published in 2021 by Recent Work Press.

About the Artist

Brian McHenry is a visual artist living on the north east coast of Ireland. He uses both digital and traditional media often incorporating text to explore the physical and emotional landscapes we inhabit during the act of remembering. He has collaborated with a range of writers, artists and musicians.

www.ingramcontent.com/pod-product-compliance
Ingram Content Group Australia Pty Ltd
76 Discovery Rd, Dandenong South VIC 3175, AU
AUHW020721050325
407891AU00005B/26